SNACKS

Tasty bites between meals

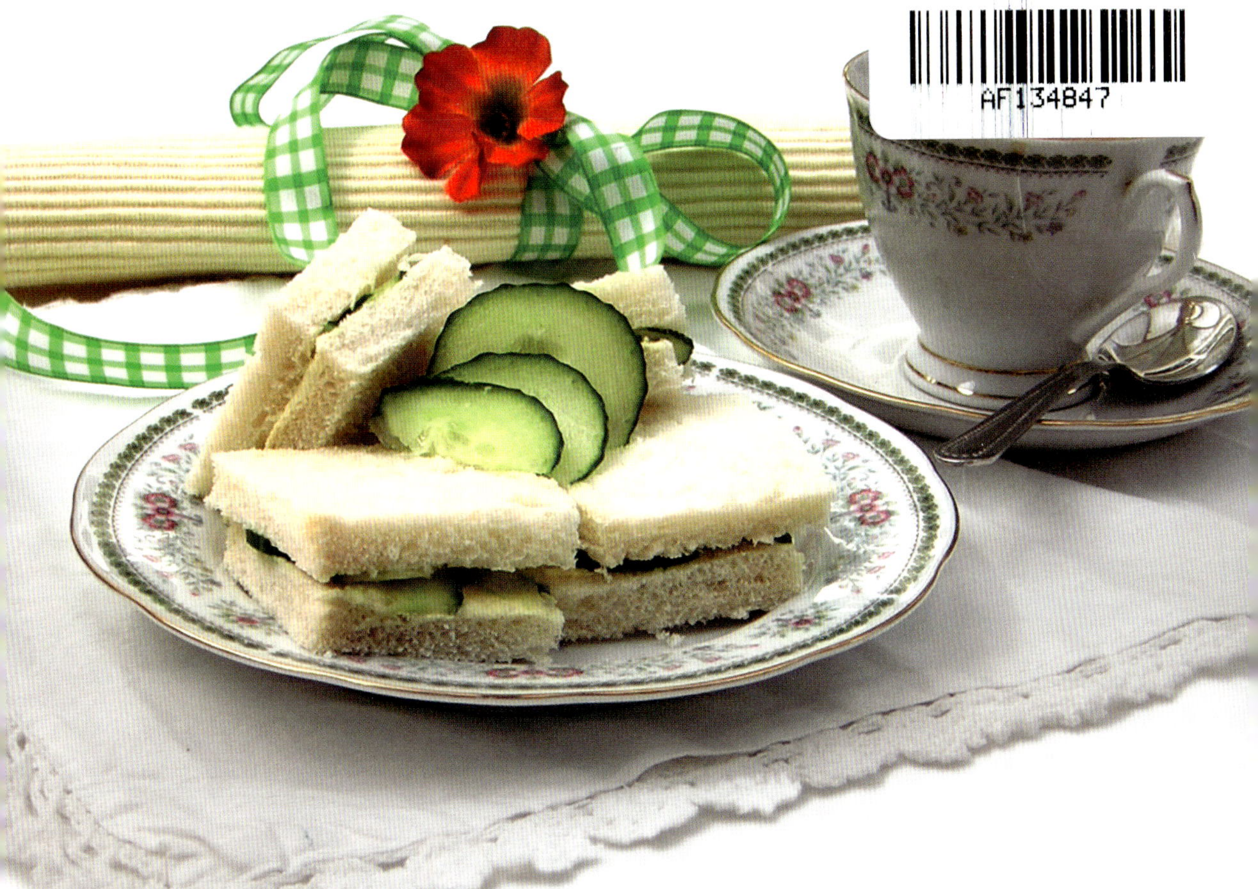

Nayna Kanabar

An imprint of
B. Jain Publishers (P) Ltd.
USA — Europe — India

Preface

From a very young age food played a very important part in my life. I was brought up in a family where food and meal times were given a lot of importance. My mother was my inspiration; I would watch and help her while she meticulously prepared elaborate meals to satisfy our palates. The dishes were mainly vegetarian Gujarati food; however immigrating to the United Kingdom introduced me to unknown ingredients; fuelling my passion for cooking and bringing me to sample fusion and multinational cuisines.

My true enthusiasm for cooking finally surfaced when I married and had a family of my own. My kitchen was my own work space; the ingredients were my tools and here I explored new flavours and textures and experimented with Asian and international cuisines. I soon realised I needed somewhere to share my recipes and my food blog **Simply Food** was set up. I cook, photograph and post recipes prepared in my kitchen on a regular basis on my blog.

From the blog an idea emerged to write a collection of recipe books, one of the topics being snacks. Being a working mum, time to prepare elaborate snacks was not always feasible and I started creating an assortment of snack recipes that were simple, versatile and quick to prepare using every day ingredients. Some recipes were basic lunchbox ideas, others perfect for appetisers and starters. Throughout all these creations my husband and two daughters have been my panel of tasters and with their help, I have selected the best 50 snack recipes to share in this book.

Publisher's Note

Snacks are often thought of as lunchbox ideas or an accompaniment to a picnic. Most of the time we all opt for unhealthy snacks instead of opting for healthy snacks to be eaten in between meals. Snacks, on the other hand, are a terrific way to eat healthy and nutritious food. It also keeps your energy levels going and do not add to your weight.

With lots of pleasure we present before you **Nayna Kanabar's** book Snacks this year. Nayna Kanabar is an accomplished cook and author. She has shared delicious and mouth-watering recipes of snacks in this book. 'Snacks' have recipes that are simple, versatile and easy to make. Her recipes are not only refreshing but are healthy too.

Snacks, an assortment of light and nutritious recipes, go beyond the average lunchbox and can be consumed as appetizers and starters. Bon appétit!

- Kuldeep Jain, CEO

Contents

Mexican Themed Recipes

- Garlic Paprika Potato Wedges 07
- Rice Salad 08
- Sprouted Moong bean salad 09
- Chilli Salsa and Wheat Tortilla Chips 10
- Scrambled Egg Tortilla wraps 12
- Avocado Dip 13
- Kidney Beans and Sweet Corn Pitta Pockets 14
- Apple and Sweet Onion Salsa 15
- Mexican Quesadillas 16

Greek Themed Recipes

- Vegetable kebabs 18
- Tropical Fruit Salad with Honey and Lime Dressing ... 19
- Chickpea and mango salad 20
- Roasted Vegetable in Pitta Bread Pocket 21
- Tzatziki Cucumber and Yoghurt Dip 22

Italian Themed Recipes

- Bruschetta 23
- Oven roasted Tomato and basil soup 24
- Penne Arrabbiata 25
- Sour Cream and Chive Dip with Vegetable Crudités ... 26

Moroccan Themed Recipes

- Moroccan Couscous Salad 27
- Moroccan Vegetarian Harira Soup 28

British Themed Recipes

- Potato chip sticks 30
- Potato skins 31
- Red Cabbage and Apple Relish 32
- Macaroni cheese 33
- Hot Ribboned omelette salad 34
- Grape and carrot salad 35
- Vegetable burgers 36
- English cucumber sandwiches 38
- Egg and cress sandwiches 39
- Toasted Cheese, Tomato and Onion Sandwich....... 40
- Kids Delight Strawberry Jam Sandwiches 41
- New Potato salad 42
- Vegetable soup 43
- Leek and potato soup 44
- Potato rosti 45

Indian/Chinese Themed Recipes

- Chilli Paneer 46
- Toasted paneer rolls 48
- Mushroom masala rolls 50
- Lentil pancakes 51
- Spinach Fritters 52

- Spicy Savoury pancakes 53
- Triple Decker Spicy Sandwich 54
- Onion Fritters 55
- Spicy potato cakes 56
- Spicy fruit salad 57
- Barbecue roasted corn salad 58

French Themed Recipes

- Green bean salad.. 59
- Cheesy Savoury French toast 60
- Onion Soup 61
- Garlic Mushrooms... 62

Index 64

Preparation time
10 minutes

Cooking time
35 minutes

Serves
4

Garlic Paprika Potato Wedges

Ingredients

4 Large baking potatoes
2 tsp Rock salt
1 tsp Paprika
½ tsp Garlic powder
½ tsp Chilli flakes
2 tbsp Olive oil

For serving:
4 tbsp Sour cream
1 tbsp Chopped chives
A pinch paprika

Method

- Wash the potatoes. Keeping the skin on, chop potatoes into chunky wedges.
- Place the potato wedges in a bowl and drizzle with olive oil and rock salt.
- Line a baking tray with kitchen foil and place the potato wedges on the tray spreading them evenly to ensure even cooking.
- Place the baking tray in a pre heated oven 200°C / 400°F for 30-35 minutes.
- In a bowl add the sour cream and finely chopped chives. Mix and transfer to a serving dish. Sprinkle with a pinch of paprika and chill in the refrigerator.
- Mix the garlic powder, chilli flakes and paprika to form a spice mixture. Keep aside.
- After 15 minutes, turn the potato wedges around to ensure even cooking. At this stage sprinkle the potato wedges with the prepared spice mixture.
- After 30 minutes, check that the wedges are cooked by inserting a skewer in them.
- Transfer the potatoes wedges to a serving tray.

Serve with sour cream and chive dip.

Oven baked crispy potato wedges seasoned with a spicy garlic paprika coating.

Preparation time
10 minutes

Cooking time
30 minutes

Serves
2

Rice Salad

Ingredients

120 gms/4 oz Cold precooked rice
120 gms/4 oz Precooked kidney beans and sweet corn
60 gms/2 oz Red and green capsicums finely diced

1 Red chilli cut into thin round slices
1 tbsp Fresh finely chopped coriander leaves
¼ tsp Salt
½ tsp White pepper powder
1 tbsp Olive oil

1 tbsp Lemon juice
For serving:
1 Red capsicum
1 Green capsicum

Method

- Put all the ingredients into a bowl and season with salt and pepper. Add the lemon juice and oil and mix thoroughly.
- Transfer to a serving dish and chill for 30 minutes.

Serve in hollowed capsicums as a starter or on its own as an accompaniment to green salad.

A colourful salad made from cold rice and Mexican vegetables. It is perfect for summer days.

Preparation time
overnight

Cooking time
10 minutes

Serves
2

Sprouted Moong Bean Salad

Ingredients

120 gms/ 4 oz Dried moong beans
2" Piece finely chopped cucumber
1 Small red onion finely chopped
1 Medium tomato finely chopped

½ tbsp Freshly chopped coriander
For dressing:
1 tbsp Lemon juice
1 tbsp Virgin olive oil

½ tsp Salt
½ tsp Fresh black pepper coarsely ground
½ tsp Red chilli flakes
2 Green chillies finely chopped

Method

- Wash and soak the moong beans for few hours. Drain them in a colander. Cover them and leave them in a dark warm place overnight for the moong beans to form sprouts. Next morning, check for sprouting. If insufficient, sprinkle a little water over the beans and leave for sprouting for additional few hours. Once the beans have sprouted fully, transfer to a tupperware container and store in the refrigerator.

- In a bowl, add 120 grams sprouted moong beans; add the chopped cucumber, tomato and onions. Toss the mixture. Add the chopped coriander. Toss again.

- In a screw top jar add all the dressing ingredients and mix thoroughly.

- Pour the dressing over the salad. Toss and mix thoroughly.

Chill salad before serving.

A healthy and very low calorie salad that is full of protein. It is refreshingly delicious with a spicy tangy dressing.

Preparation time	Resting time (for dough)	Cooking time	Serves
15 minutes	30 minutes	40 minutes	4

Chilli Salsa & Wheat Tortilla Chips

Ingredients

For chilli salsa:
4 Medium tomatoes
1 Long, sweet, red chilli pepper
1 tsp Cumin powder
1 tsp Salt

½ tsp Fresh garlic paste
3 Green chillies
3 Sprigs fresh coriander
½ tsp Paprika powder
1 tbsp Lemon juice

For wheat tortilla chips:
240 gms/8 oz Whole wheat flour
½ tsp Salt
2 tbsp Olive oil
1 tsp Baking powder

Water to make dough
600 ml/20 fl oz Sunflower oil for deep frying

Method

For chilli salsa:

- Cut a cross on top of the tomatoes and plunge them into boiling water for 3 minutes.
- Remove the tomatoes from the water and plunge into ice cold water and peel the skin off.
- Roughly chop the tomatoes.
- Remove the stalk and seeds from the sweet red chilli pepper and chop roughly.
- Put the pepper in a blender jug; add the salt, garlic, paprika powder, green chillies, cumin powder and lemon juice. Blend coarsely. Add the chopped tomatoes and blend again, only for a few seconds; the chilli salsa should have a coarse texture. Transfer to a serving dish and garnish with fresh chopped coriander.

For wheat tortilla chips:

- In a bowl, add wheat flour, salt, baking powder and olive oil.
- Add water sparingly to the flour and mix till the flour comes together to form a soft, pliable dough.
- Cover and keep the dough aside for 30 minutes to rest.
- Heat a skillet. While it is heating, divide the dough into 10 walnut sized balls and using some dry flour for dusting, roll out round disc shapes approximately 8 inches in diameter.
- Cook the tortillas on the skillet first one side and then the other till brown spots appear on them.
- Remove cooked tortillas from the skillet and repeat procedure for the remaining dough.
- To make the tortilla chips, stack the cooked tortillas one on top of another and cut into halves, quarters and then eighths to form triangular pieces.
- Heat oil in a frying pan and deep fry tortilla triangles till golden brown and crisp.
- Drain the tortilla chips on kitchen paper. Once cool, store in an air tight container to retain crispness.

Serve tortilla chips with the chilli salsa.

Mexican tortillas with zingy chilli salsa, makes a perfect snack for parties or simply to enjoy anytime of the day.

Preparation time
10 minutes

Cooking time
10 minutes

Serves
4

Scrambled Egg Tortilla Wraps

Ingredients

3 Eggs
2 tbsp Pre cooked black eyed beans
2 tbsp Sour cream
¼ tsp Salt & pepper each
1 tbsp Finely chopped spring onion

2 Finely chopped green chillies
1 De-seeded and finely chopped tomato
2 Finely chopped button mushrooms
1 tbsp Freshly chopped coriander
4 Wheat tortillas

1 Knob Butter
1 tbsp Olive oil
Shredded lettuce leaves

Method

- In a bowl, break the eggs, add salt, pepper, green chillies and sour cream, beat together.
- In a frying pan add the butter and olive oil and heat. When it is hot, add the mushrooms and spring onions and sauté for one minute. Add the tomatoes, black eyed beans and sauté for another minute.
- Add the egg mixture and stir constantly. Scrambled eggs are cooked when most of the egg mixture has set. Do not over cook the eggs as this will separate them. Stir in the chopped coriander.
- Heat a skillet and warm the tortilla wraps one at a time.
- Spoon the egg mixture on the centre of the warmed tortilla wrap. Add on top some shredded lettuce leaves and roll it up.
- Repeat for the remaining tortillas.

Serve hot with tomato ketchup or brown sauce.

Wheat tortilla wraps filled with wholesome scrambled eggs.

Preparation time
10 minutes

Cooking time
10 minutes

Serves
2

Avocado dip

Ingredients

- 1 Ripe avocado
- 1 tbsp Lemon juice
- ¼ tsp Salt
- ¼ tsp Pepper
- 2 Spring onions finely chopped
- 1 Green chilli finely chopped
- ½ tbsp Finely chopped fresh coriander
- ½ tsp garlic paste

Method

- Cut the avocado in half and remove the seed. Scoop all the flesh out of the avocados using a spoon and place the flesh into a bowl.
- Using a fork, mash the avocado, add the finely chopped spring onions, chilli, garlic and chopped coriander. Mix well.
- Season the avocado mixture with salt and pepper and add the lemon juice.
- Transfer to a serving bowl cover and chill for 1 hour before serving.

Serve with breadsticks or tortilla chips.

Creamy rich avocado dip with subtle hint of garlic and lemon.

Preparation time
5 minutes

Cooking time
15 minutes

Serves
4

Kidney Beans and Sweet Corn Pitta Pockets

Ingredients

240 gms/8 oz Precooked kidney beans
120 gms/4 oz Precooked sweet corn kernels
½ tsp Salt
½ tsp Chilli powder
½ tsp Turmeric powder

¼ tsp Cumin powder
¼ tsp Coriander powder
1 tbsp Tomato puree
4 tbsp Water
1 tbsp Olive oil

For serving:
4 Pitta bread
1 Bowl mixed salad-shredded lettuce, diced cucumber, grated carrot and diced tomato

Method

- Heat the oil in a pan, when it is hot add the kidney beans and sweet corn kernels, sauté for 3 minutes.
- Mix the tomato puree with water, add to the kidney beans and sweet corn mixture in the pan.
- Add salt, turmeric powder, chilli powder, cumin powder, coriander powder and cook the mixture for 3-4 minutes until spices infuse into the mixture and until it is almost dry. Remove from heat.
- Place the pitta bread in the toaster to warm up but do not make them crispy.
- Cut each pitta bread in half and open out to form a pocket. Spoon the prepared kidney bean and sweet corn filling into the pockets.

Serve hot accompanied with a side salad.

A fast and easy lunch snack that is wholesome and nutritious.

Preparation time
10 minutes

Cooking time
10-15 minutes

Serves
2

Apple and Sweet Onion Salsa

Ingredients

1 Medium red onion
1 Crisp red / green apple
60 grams / 2 oz Diced mixed peppers
2" Piece of cucumber

Dressing:
½ tsp Fresh ginger paste
2 tbsp Lemon juice
1 tbsp White wine vinegar

½ tsp Salt
¼ tsp Cumin powder
¼ tsp Cayenne pepper

Method

- Peel and finely slice the onion and put it into a bowl.
- Keep the skin on the cucumber and finely dice it, add it to the onions.
- Core the apple and keeping the skin on dice it finely and add it to the bowl.
- Add the diced peppers to the bowl.
- Take a jar with a lid and add the ginger paste, lemon juice, vinegar, salt, cumin powder and cayenne pepper. Close the lid and shake the jar to make the dressing.
- Pour the dressing over the vegetables in the bowl and toss to coat everything with the dressing.
- Transfer salsa to a serving bowl.

Serve with tortilla chips or crackers.

A colourful salsa with a combination of fruit and vegetables with a tangy vinaigrette dressing.

Preparation time
20 minutes

Cooking time
10 minutes

Serves
2

Mexican Quesadillas

Ingredients

60 gms / 2 oz Grated cheddar cheese

60 gms / 2 oz Precooked sweet corn kernels

90 gms / 3 oz Finely diced mixed peppers (red/green/yellow)

1 Spring onion finely chopped

4 Wheat tortillas

For salsa:

3 Firm tomatoes

1 tablespoon Chilli sauce

1 tbsp Tomato ketchup

½ tsp Salt

½ tsp Paprika

1 red Chilli finely sliced

1 tbsp Freshly chopped coriander

Method

To make salsa:

- Cut a diagonal cross on top of each tomato and put them into boiling water for 3 minutes.
- Remove tomatoes from the boiling water and plunge them into iced water.
- Remove tomatoes from iced water and peel the skin off and cut into halves.
- Remove the seeds and finely dice the tomatoes and add to a bowl.
- To the diced tomatoes add chilli sauce, tomato sauce, salt, paprika, chilli and fresh coriander and mix thoroughly. Keep aside.

Making the quesadillas:

- Heat a skillet and when it is hot place a tortilla wrap on it. Reduce heat to medium.
- Spread some tomato salsa on to the tortilla and sprinkle with grated cheese.
- Once the cheese starts to melt sprinkle on top of it the spring onions, sweet corn and peppers.
- Cover the tortilla with the second wrap and using spatula press gently so that the filling is sandwiched between the two wraps. Cook on medium heat for a minute.
- After 1 minute, carefully flip the tortilla wrap to cook the top side.
- Gently press the wrap with a spatula and cook for 1 more minute till cheese is totally melted.
- Remove the tortilla sandwich from the skillet and place on a dish.
- Cut into quarters and transfer to a serving dish.
- Repeat for any remaining wraps.

Serve quesadillas with sour cream and chive dip.

Wholesome wheat tortilla wraps with a spicy salsa and melted cheese filling.

Preparation time
15 minutes

Marinating time
3 hours

Cooking time
5-10 minutes

Serves
7

Vegetable Kebabs

Ingredients

240 gms/8 oz Diced paneer (Indian Cheese)
240 gms/8 oz Mixed red/green/yellow capsicum pieces
12 Cherry tomatoes
1 Red onion cut into chunks
6 Small button mushrooms

For Marinade:
1 tsp Fresh garlic paste
1 tsp Fresh ginger paste
1 tsp Green chilli paste
2 tbsp Yoghurt
1 tsp Salt
1 tbsp Tandoori masala paste
1 tbsp Lemon juice
1 tbsp Olive oil

NB - Tandoori masala paste-garam masala, garlic powder, ginger powder, cumin powder, cayenne pepper, oil

Method

- Soak 8 wooden skewers in water (this ensures that they don't burn while grilling the kebabs).
- In a large bowl add all the ingredients in the marinade list and mix thoroughly.
- Add the paneer cubes, capsicums, mushrooms, onions and cherry tomatoes. Toss them in the mixture to coat everything evenly.
- Cover and refrigerate for 2-3 hours.

Serve hot with yoghurt, mint chutney and lemon wedges.
NB- This dish can be prepared using Tofu / Quorn instead of Paneer.

- Once paneer and vegetables are marinated, prepare the skewers for grilling. Thread the wooden skewers alternating paneer and different vegetables. Prepare all skewers in this way.
- Place skewers on an oiled baking tray and place under medium hot grill, turning them frequently till paneer and vegetables are slightly charred and cooked. Alternatively, these vegetable kebabs can be cooked on a barbeque.

Paneer and vegetables marinated in aromatic spices and grilled to perfection. A wonderful option for barbeques.

Tropical Fruit Salad with Honey and Lime Dressing

Preparation time 20 minutes

Chilling time 30 minutes

Serves 4

Ingredients

2 Mangoes
2 Nectarines
3 Yellow plums

2 White guava
1 Blood red orange

For dressing:
60 ml/2 fl oz/¼ cup Fresh orange juice
1 tsp Lime zest

½ tsp Lemon zest
2 tbsp Honey
1 tbsp Lime juice

Method

- Peel the mango and dice into cubes.
- Halve the nectarines and remove the deseed. Cut into small pieces.
- Halve the plums and remove the deseed. Cut into small pieces.
- Peel the guava and cut into small pieces.
- Peel the orange and cut into segments.
- Place all the prepared fruit into a serving bowl.
- In a clean jar add all the dressing ingredients and screw on the lid. Shake the jar to combine the dressing ingredients.
- Pour the dressing over the fruit salad. Toss the fruit salad to coat the fruit with the dressing.
- Chill the fruit salad before serving.

Serve for breakfast or lunch as a starter with a spoonful of fromage frais.

A colourful and vibrant fruit salad dressed with a refreshing lime and honey dressing.

Note: Any seasonal fruit can be used in the fruit salad.

Preparation time
15 minutes

Cooking time
10 minutes

Serves
2

Chickpea and Mango Salad

Ingredients

1 Firm ripe mango deseeded and diced
120 gms/4 oz Cooked white chickpeas
120 gms/4 oz Shredded iceberg lettuce leaves

12 Cherry tomatoes cut into quarters
60 gms/2 oz Red/green capsicums finely diced
Lemon wedges for serving

For dressing:
2 tbsp Natural yoghurt
1 tsp Mint sauce
A pinch each Salt and black pepper

Method

- In a bowl, add the mango, shredded lettuce, chickpeas, cherry tomatoes and the diced capsicums. Mix all the salad ingredients.
- In another bowl add the yoghurt, mint sauce, salt and pepper. Combine to form a dressing.
- Pour the dressing over the salad and toss to coat all the salad ingredients.
- Transfer to a serving dish and serve with lemon wedges.

Serve with toasted pitta bread.

Tropical mango and chickpeas dressed with a simple mint and yoghurt dressing giving freshness to this wonderful salad.

Preparation time
15 minutes

Cooking time
20 minutes

Serves
2

Roasted Vegetables in Pitta Bread Pockets

Ingredients

1/2 Red capsicum cut into 2.5 cm pieces
1/2 Green capsicum cut into 2.5 cm pieces
2 Mushrooms cut into slices
1 Red onion cut into chunks
1 Courgette cut into 2.5 cm slices
2 tbsp Olive oil
2 Pitta breads
A pinch sea salt and coarsely ground black pepper
2 tbsp Hot chilli scuce
1 Bowl of mixed side salad; shredded lettuce, diced cucumber, grated carrots and tomato slices

Method

- Place all the vegetables on a baking tray and drizzle with olive oil.
- Generously sprinkle the vegetables with coarsely ground black pepper and sea salt.
- Bake the vegetables in a preheated oven at 200°C/400°F for 20 minutes.

Serve immediately with a side salad.

- Heat pitta bread in a pan and slit the tops to form pockets. Fill the pitta bread with the roasted vegetables and top with hot chilli sauce, if desired.

Oven roasted vegetables served in an open pitta bread. A warm sandwich that is perfect for lunch.

Preparation time
10 minutes
(+ 1 hour straining time)

Cooking time
10-15 minutes

Chilling time
1 hour

Serves
2

Tzatziki cucumber and yoghurt dip

Ingredients

250 ml / 8 oz Natural yoghurt
½ Cucumber
½ tsp salt
1 tsp Extra virgin olive oil
2 Cloves garlic

Method

- Place a strainer over a bowl and pour natural yoghurt into it. Leave it for 1 hour or until all the water has drained from the yoghurt.
- Peel the cucumber and cut in half, remove the seeds and finely dice the cucumber.
- Place the diced cucumber in another strainer over a bowl and sprinkle it with salt to draw out surplus liquid from the cucumber.
- Peel the garlic and finely mince it to a smooth paste.
- In a bowl, add the drained yoghurt and drained cucumber. Discard the surplus drained liquids.
- Add the garlic and olive oil to the yoghurt and cucumber mixture in the bowl and mix well. Transfer to a serving bowl.
- Cover and refrigerate for 1 hour before serving

Serve with warm toasted pitta bread.

A creamy yoghurt and cucumber dip flavoured with garlic and extra virgin olive oil.

Preparation time
15 minutes

Cooking time
10 minutes

Serves
4

Bruschetta

Ingredients

1 Long french bread stick
2 Large beef tomatoes or 6 medium tomatoes
1 Small red onion
2 Cloves of garlic
¼ tsp Pepper
¼ tsp Salt
10 Basil leaves
2 tbsp Extra virgin olive oil

Method

- Cut a cross on top of each tomato and put in boiling water for 3 minutes.
- After three minutes remove tomatoes from hot water and plunge them into cold water to stop the cooking process.
- Remove tomatoes from cold water and peel their skin off.
- Cut the tomatoes in half and discard the seeds. Dice the tomatoes and keep aside.
- Peel and chop the onion very finely and keep aside.
- Cut diagonally 8 slices, each one inch thick from french bread.
- Place under a hot grill and toast both sides of the bread.
- Remove toasted bread from the grill and rub the top side with the peeled garlic to infuse a garlic flavour to the bread. Drizzle with a little olive oil on top of the toasted bread slices.
- Place the toasted bread slices on to a serving platter and top with the chopped tomatoes followed by the chopped onions. Season with salt and pepper. Tear the basil leaves and garnish on top.
- Drizzle with a little more olive oil and serve immediately.

Serve with hot soup.

A simple appetizer which is perfect for parties as biting food or as a starter or lunch dish.

Preparation time
5 minutes

Cooking time
35 minutes

Serves
4

Oven Roasted Tomato and Basil Soup

Ingredients

- 12 Medium tomatoes washed and halved
- 2 tbsp Olive oil
- 1 Small onion finely chopped
- 1 Garlic clove finely minced
- 10 Basil leaves for soup
- 4 Basil leaves for garnish
- ½ tsp Salt
- ½ tsp Black pepper
- 2 tbsp Single cream
- 500 ml/16 fl oz Water

Method

- Place the tomatoes on a baking tray and grizzle with a little olive oil. Sprinkle with salt and pepper.
- Place the tray in the hot oven at 200°C or 400°F for 20 minutes.
- In a pan, add 1 tbsp of olive oil and heat it. Add the garlic and onions. Sauté till translucent.
- Remove the roasted tomatoes from the oven and add them to the pan of garlic and onions. Add 500 ml water. Bring soup to a boil.
- Tear the basil leaves and add to the soup. Add sugar and season it with salt and pepper. Simmer for 5 minutes.
- After 5 minutes transfer the soup to a blender and blend to a smooth puree. Strain the soup to remove any tomato seeds.
- Return soup to the pan and heat thoroughly again.
- Pour the soup into soup bowls and swirl cream over the top. Garnish with a basil leaf.

Serve with hot, crusty bread rolls.

Hearty tomato soup delicately infused with basil, rich and creamy making it a perfect starter for any meal.

Preparation time
15 minutes

Cooking time
30 minutes

Serves
2

Penne Arrabbiata

Ingredients

For pasta:
240 gms / 8 oz Uncooked pasta penne
1 tsp salt
1 tsp olive oil
2 litres Water

For sauce:
60 gms / 2 oz Precooked sweet corn kernels
60 gms / 2 oz mixed Peppers red /green / yellow diced
1 Small onion finely diced
60 gms / 2 oz Courgettes finely diced
250 ml Passata (sieved tomatoes)
1 tsp Salt
1 tsp Sugar
2 tsp Dried Italian spice (oregano)
½ tsp Black pepper powder
2 Chillies finely chopped
1 Clove garlic finely chopped
1 tbsp Olive oil

Method

- In a pan, heat the olive oil and add the onions and garlic. Sauté till translucent.
- Add the passata and cook sauce for 2-3 minutes.
- Add the peppers, sweet corn, courgettes to the tomato sauce and cook till vegetables are tender.
- Add the salt and pepper, Italian spice, chillies and sugar and simmer sauce on low heat till sauce thickens. Remove from heat and keep aside.
- Heat water in a large saucepan, when it comes to a boil add 1 teaspoon salt and the penne pasta.
- Reduce heat to simmer and cook pasta until al dente. (al dente means its cooked but it still has a bite and it is not overcooked and mushy.)
- Drain the pasta and return it to saucepan, add 1 teaspoon olive oil and stir it into the pasta.

To serve put boiled pasta into a bowl and top with the Arrabbiata sauce. Garnish with parmesan shavings if desired.

Italian vegetable pasta penne, cooked in a spicy hot tomato sauce with vegetables, seasoned richly with aromatic Italian mixed herbs and garlic.

Preparation time
5 minutes
(+ 1 hour straining time)

Cooking time
10 minutes

Chilling time
1 hour

Serves
2

Sour Cream and Chive Dip

Ingredients

125 ml Sour cream
1 tbsp Fresh finely chopped chives
Pinch of salt
Pinch of white pepper
1 Clove garlic finely chopped

Method

- In a bowl add sour cream, garlic and chives. Mix well.
- Season with salt and pepper.
- Transfer to a serving bowl and garish with few chopped chives.
- Chill for 1 hour.

Serve with vegetable crudités.

Creamy sour cream dip with a peppery taste of chives and a hint of garlic.

Preparation time
30 minutes

Cooking time
15-20 minutes

Serves
4

Moroccan Couscous Salad

Ingredients

- 120 gms / 4 oz Dry instant couscous
- 3" Piece cucumber diced
- 2 Tomato deseeded and diced
- 3 Spring onions finely sliced
- 1 Medium carrot grated
- ½ Red pepper finely diced
- ½ Green pepper finely diced
- 12 Seedless grapes cut in halves
- 1 tbsp Jalapeno peppers in brine (bottled)
- 1 tbsp Fresh chopped coriander for garnishing
- 1 tbsp Sultanas
- 4 Lemon wedges for garnishing

For dressing:
- Juice of ½ a lime
- ½ tsp Lime zest
- ¾ tsp Salt
- ½ tsp White pepper powder
- 1 tbsp Olive oil
- 1 tbsp Brine (from bottled jalapenos)
- 2 tsp Tobasco sauce (hot red pepper sauce)

Method

- Add the dry couscous to a large bowl. Add enough boiling water to just cover the dry couscous. Cover and leave for 15 minutes or until the couscous has soaked up all the water. Once couscous is ready, fluff it up with a fork and leave to cool.
- In a jar with a lid add all the dressing ingredients. Shake and keep aside.
- Add the dressing to the cooled couscous and stir in.
- Mix together diced cucumber, tomato, carrots, spring onions, peppers and grapes. Add this to the prepared couscous and toss together.
- Transfer the couscous salad to a serving platter and sprinkle with jalapeno peppers and sultanas.
- Garnish with fresh coriander.

Serve immediately with hot crusty bread or pitta bread and lemon wedges.

Colourful textured salad with a rainbow of vibrant colours and Middle Eastern flavours.

Preparation time	Cooking time	Serves
10 minutes	**30 minutes**	**4**

Moroccan Vegetarian Harira Soup

Ingredients

For soup:

240 gms / 8 oz Precooked white chickpeas
2 Medium potatoes
1 Small onion finely chopped
1 tbsp Finely chopped fresh coriander
3 Tomatoes deseeded and finely chopped
½ tsp Fresh ginger paste
½ tsp Fresh garlic paste
½ tsp Cumin powder
½ tsp Coriander powder
½ tsp Ground cinnamon
½ tsp Turmeric powder
1½ tsp Salt
1 tbsp Harissa paste
2 tbsp Olive oil
1 litre Water

For harissa paste:

6 Red dried chillies
2 Cloves garlic
½ tsp Cumin powder
½ tsp Coriander powder
¼ tsp Salt
1 tsp Olive oil
30 ml Hot water

Method

Make the harissa paste:

- Add hot water to dried chillies and leave for 30 minutes.
- Place the soaked chillies together with the garlic, cumin, coriander, salt and olive oil into a blender and blend to make a fine smooth paste. Transfer this paste into a sterilised jar and refrigerate for future use. You will not need to use all this paste for the recipe.

Making the soup:

- Heat oil in a pan and sauté the onions and the garlic till soft and translucent.
- Add the ginger and tomatoes and sauté for a few more minutes. Add the cumin powder and the coriander powder, turmeric, and salt. Sauté till spices blend into the tomatoes.
- Add the potatoes and chickpeas followed by 1 litre of water and bring the soup to a boil. Reduce heat and simmer for 20 minutes till potatoes are soft and cooked.
- Stir in the cinnamon and 1 tablespoon of the Harissa sauce. Adjust seasoning as required.
- Stir in the freshly chopped coriander leaves.

Serve the soup with pitta bread.

A wonderful spicy chickpea and potato soup with aromatic flavours of Morocco.

Preparation time
15 minutes

Cooking time
40 minutes

Serves
2

Potato Chip Sticks

Ingredients

2 Large potatoes
½ tsp Salt
½ tsp Chilli powder
500 ml/16 fl oz Sunflower oil for frying

Method

- Peel and wash the potatoes. Cut them in fine juliennes (fine thin strips).
- Separate and spread the julienned potatoes on to a tea towel and pat them totally dry.
- Heat the oil in a large pan and deep fry potato juliennes in small batches on medium heat till golden brown (do not be tempted to cook them on a high flame as this will result in soggy chip sticks.)
- Drain on kitchen paper. If fried at the correct temperature, potato chip sticks will be crunchy when they cool. Repeat for remaining potatoes.

To serve, sprinkle with salt and chilli powder.

Surplus can be stored in an air tight container.

A delectable crunchy potato snack that you will not be able to stop munching.

Preparation time
10 minutes

Cooking time
20 minutes

Serves
4

Potato Skins

Ingredients

2 Potatoes (medium in size)	¾ tsp Salt	2 tbsp Cooked sweet corn kernels	1 tsp Butter
120 gms/4 oz Cheddar cheese	2 Spring onions finely chopped	1 tbsp Chilli sauce	½ tsp White pepper powder

Method

- Wash and prick the potatoes. Cook in a microwave on high flame for approximately 15-20 minutes. Check that they are cooked inside by pricking them with a skewer.
- When potatoes are cooked, cut into halves.
- Scoop out some of the flesh from the potato halves leaving some potato on the skin so that potato shells remain intact.
- Put all the scooped potato flesh into a bowl. Add the onions, sweet corn, salt, pepper, chilli sauce, butter and two ounces of cheese and mix thoroughly.
- Place the potato skins on a baking tray and spoon the prepared potato mixture into the skins.
- Sprinkle with remaining cheese and bake in a pre heated oven at 200°C / 400°F for 20 minutes till cheese melts and turns golden brown.
- Remove from oven and transfer to a serving dish.

Serve hot with a salad.

Potato skins filled with a savoury spicy filling, topped with cheese and baked until golden brown and crisp.

Preparation time
10 minutes

Cooking time
10 minutes

Serves
4

Red Cabbage & Apple Relish

Ingredients

240 gms/8 oz Finely shredded red cabbage
¼ Finely sliced red onion
1 Granny smith apple, cored and grated with skin on (this recipe works best with sharp apples)

4 Finely sliced Green chillies
¾ tsp Salt
¼ tsp Mustard seeds
¼ tsp Fenugreek seeds

1 tbsp Mild olive oil
½ tsp Sugar
Juice of half a lemon

Method

- Heat oil in a pan and when hot add the mustard seeds and fenugreek seeds.
- Add the cabbage, onion and apples. Stir fry for 3-4 minutes.
- Add the green chillies, lemon juice, sugar and salt.
- Stir fry for 5 more minutes till cabbage just wilts but still retains the crunchiness.
- Transfer to a serving dish.

To serve, spoon generously on freshly toasted French bread slices.

A tangy spicy relish ideal as a sandwich filling, served on an open sandwich, rolled in a roti or stirred in some curd rice.

Preparation time
5 minutes

Cooking time
35 minutes

Serves
4

Macaroni Cheese

Ingredients

240 gms/8 oz Macaroni
1 tsp Olive oil
1 tsp Salt for boiling

60 gms/2 oz Bread crumbs
For white sauce:
30 gms /1 oz Butter

30 gms /1 oz Plain flour
600 ml/20 fl oz Milk
240 gms/8 oz Grated cheddar cheese

Salt for sauce
½ tsp Pepper
A pinch nutmeg

Method

- Heat water in a large pan and add 1 tsp salt when it starts to boil. Add the macaroni and cook for 8-10 minutes till it is al dente. Drain the macaroni and return to the pan. Add 1 tsp olive oil and toss. Transfer to a shallow, oven proof dish. Cover and keep aside.
- Add butter to a pan and allow it to melt. Add the flour and stir for few minutes making a roux. Gradually whisk in the milk, a little at a time. Cook for 10-15 minutes till sauce thickens to dropping consistency. Season the sauce with salt, pepper and nutmeg.
- Add half the cheese and stir it into the sauce until it melts.
- Pour the sauce over the precooked macaroni and stir it in. Sprinkle the bread crumbs and remainder of cheese on top of the macaroni and place the dish in a hot, preheated grill till the cheese turns brown.
- Remove from grill and serve immediately with fresh salad.

Creamy white sauce delicately enhanced with a subtle flavour of nutmeg, coating the macaroni which is topped with a crispy golden brown cheese and bread crumb crust.

Preparation time
15 minutes

Cooking time
10 minutes

Serves
2

Hot Ribboned Omelette Salad

Ingredients

For omelette:
2 Eggs
2 tbsp Milk
¼ tsp Salt
¼ tsp Pepper
½ tsp Tabasco sauce
1 tbsp Olive oil
1 Green chilli finely chopped

For salad:
1 Courgette
1 Carrot
½ Red capsicum
1 tbsp Finely chopped fresh coriander
1 tbsp Olive oil
Parmesan shavings

Method

- Julienne (cut into fine strips) the courgette, carrot and capsicum. Keep aside.
- In a frying pan, add olive oil and let it heat. When hot, add the julienned vegetables and stir fry for 1 minute. Remove the vegetables from the pan and keep aside.
- In a bowl, break the eggs, add milk, salt, pepper, chilli and Tabasco sauce. Mix together.
- In the frying pan put 1 tbsp of oil and allow to heat. Pour the egg mixture into the pan and swirl around to form an omelette.
- When omelette is cooked underneath flip to cook the top side.
- Remove the cooked omelette from the frying pan and cut into thin strips.
- In a bowl add the stir fried vegetables together with the strips of omelette. Add coriander and toss together.
- Transfer to a serving dish and sprinkle with parmesan shavings.

Serve hot with warm bread rolls.

A colourful, easy to make, mouth watering and simple warm salad with easily available ingredients.

Preparation time
10 minutes

Cooking time
10 minutes

Serves
1

Grape and Carrot Salad

Ingredients

20 Red seedless grapes cut into halves

1 Medium carrot peeled and shredded

30 gms/1 oz Roasted salted peanuts

1 tbsp Fresh chopped coriander

For dressing:

30 gms/1 oz Roasted, salted peanuts coarsely ground

½ tsp Lemon zest

1 tbsp Lemon juice

Pinch of Chilli flakes

Method

- In a bowl add the grape halves, shredded carrot, chopped coriander and roasted peanuts. Mix all the salad ingredients.
- In another bowl add the coarsely ground peanuts, chilli flakes, lemon zest and the lemon juice. Combine to form a dressing.
- Pour the dressing over the salad and toss to coat all the salad ingredients.
- Transfer to a serving dish and serve immediately as a starter.

Serve with toasted pitta bread.

A simple salad, with a sweet and tangy flavour enhanced with the crunch of roasted peanuts.

Preparation time	Cooking time	Serves
25 minutes	30 minutes	4

Vegetable Burgers

Ingredients

2 Medium potatoes
120 gms/4 oz Frozen green peas
2 small Carrots
120 gms/4 oz Frozen sweet corn
2 Green chillies finely chopped
1 tsp Salt
½ tsp Chilli flakes

1 tbsp Lemon juice
2 tsp Cornflour
4 tbsp Bread crumbs
2 tbsp Bread crumbs for coating burgers
1 Egg
2 tbsp Sunflower oil for shallow frying

For serving:
8 Small burger buns
2 tbsp Mayonnaise
Mixed salad-lettuce, cucumber slices, tomato slices and onion rings

Method

- Peel and grate the potatoes and carrots.
- Coarsely grind the peas and sweet corn.
- In a microwaveable bowl, add 3 tbsp of water. Add the potatoes, carrots, peas and sweet corn. Cook covered in the microwave for 6-8 minutes till vegetables are cooked and tender.
- Remove vegetables from the microwave and drain any excess water. Coarsely mash the vegetable mixture. Add the salt, chillies, chilli flakes and lemon juice. Leave aside to cool.
- Once cooled, add 4 tbsp bread crumbs and mix in.
- Divide mixture into 8 parts and roll into lemon sized balls. Flatten the balls to give a burger shape.
- Take 3 dishes, in the first dish, place the cornflour, beat the egg and pour it into the second dish. In the third dish place the bread crumbs.
- Take the burger patties. First coat them in cornflour on both sides, shake off the excess and then dip in the beaten egg. Finally, dip the burger pattie in bread crumbs ensuring that its top, bottom and sides are fully coated with the bread crumbs.
- Pat the burger pattie gently in the palm of your hands so the bread crumbs stick to the pattie.
- Repeat for the remaining burger patties.
- When all the burger patties are covered in bread crumbs, place them on a baking tray and chill for 30 minutes. It is important to ensure that the patties don't fall apart while frying.
- After 30 minutes, shallow fry patties in small batches on both sides till they turn golden brown, alternately, for a healthier option, the burger patties can be sprayed with cooking oil and placed under hot grill to cook on each side.
- Cut the burger buns in half and place on a serving dish.
- Place some shredded lettuce leaves on the bottom half, top with the cooked burger pattie. Place cucumber, tomato and onion rings on top of the burger followed by a dollop of mayonnaise. Place the other half of the bun to cover.

Serve immediately with potato fries.

Fresh vegetables cooked and flavoured in a blend of mild aromatic spices. Shaped to form mini vegetable burgers.

Preparation time
10 minutes

Cooking time
10 minutes

Serves
2

English Cucumber Sandwiches

Ingredients

8 Fresh white bread slices   4" piece Cucumber   1 tbsp Softened butter

Method

- Pile the bread slices on top of each other and remove crusts from all four sides.
- Butter all the bread slices on one side and keep aside.
- Slice the cucumber very thinly into round slices.
- Place two slices of bread on a tray, buttered side up. Place a few slices of cucumber on it. Cover with the second slice of bread buttered side down to make a sandwich.
- Cut the sandwich into 4 quarters and place on a serving tray. Repeat for the remaining bread slices.

Serve with a hot cup of English tea.

Dainty and soft cucumber sandwiches that are a must for any afternoon tea.

Preparation time
20 minutes

Cooking time
40 minutes

Serves
4

Egg and Cress Sandwiches

Ingredients

8 Slices wholemeal bread
2 Hard boiled eggs

1 tbsp Mayonnaise
1 Bunch cress

A pinch of salt & pepper

Method

- Pile the bread slices on top of each other and remove crusts from all four sides.
- Chop up the eggs coarsely and add the mayonnaise. Season with salt and pepper and combine to make a coarse mixture.
- Place two slices of bread on a tray. Spoon the prepared egg mixture over the bread slices and sprinkle the cress on top. Cover with the second slice of bread to make a sandwich.
- Cut the sandwich into 4 triangles and place on a serving tray. Repeat for the remaining bread slices. Garnish with remaining cress.

Serve with a hot cup of English tea.

Healthy brown bread topped with a delicious egg and cress filling.

Preparation time
5 minutes

Cooking time
6 minutes

Serves
2

Toasted Cheese, Tomato and Onion Sandwich

Ingredients

4 slices White bread
60 gms/2 oz Cheddar grated cheese
1 Small red onion thinly sliced
1 Tomato thinly sliced
1 tbsp Butter
A pinch of salt and pepper

Method

- Butter all four slices of bread.
- In a double sandwich toaster, place two slices of bread side by side, buttered side down.
- Put the grated cheese on the slice. Top with onion slices followed by tomato slices.
- Season with a pinch of salt and pepper.
- Cover with the remaining two slices, buttered side up.
- Cover and toast the sandwiches for 4-5 minutes till they turn golden brown.
- Remove the toasted sandwich from the toaster and cut each into two triangles.

Serve hot with tomato ketchup.

Hot toasted cheesy sandwiches with tomato and onion.

Preparation time
5 minutes

Cooking time
5-7 minutes

Serves
2

Kids Delight – Strawberry Jam Sandwich

Ingredients

4 White bread slices   2 tbsp Strawberry jam   1/2 tbsp Butter

Method

- Using a round cookie cutter, cut out 4 bread circles from each slice of bread (in total 16 circles).
- Spread jam on 8 of the circles and butter on the remaining 8 bread circles.
- For making the sandwich, one jam circle is pressed with one butter circle. Place sandwiches on a serving platter.

Serve with a glass of cold milkshake.

A delightful fast and easy sandwich that is simple and tasty. It is a perfect tea time snack.

Preparation time
10 minutes

Cooking time
25 minutes

Serves
4

New Potato Salad

Ingredients

480 gms/16 oz Baby potatoes
4 Spring onions finely chopped
1 tbsp Chives finely chopped
1 tbsp White wine vinegar

1 tbsp Extra virgin olive oil
2 tbsp Mayonnaise
2 tbsp Crème fraiche
½ tsp White pepper powder

½ tsp Chilli flakes
1 tsp Salt

Method

- Wash the baby potatoes and boil them with the skin on in a pan of water for approximately 20-25 minutes. Check to see that the potatoes are cooked and tender but not mushy; they should be holding their shape.
- Drain the potatoes and return to the pan. Drizzle the hot cooked potatoes with olive oil and vinegar. Season with salt. Cover and keep aside.
- In a bowl add the mayonnaise, crème fraiche, pepper powder, chilli flakes and a pinch of salt. Mix thoroughly.
- Reserve a little of the spring onions and chives for garnishing and fold the remainder of spring onions and chives into the mayonnaise mixture.
- Add this mayonnaise dressing to the warm seasoned potatoes. Toss to coat all the potatoes with this dressing.
- Transfer to a serving dish and garnish with remaining chives and spring onions.

Potato salad can be served warm or cold as an accompaniment to a fresh green salad.

Boiled baby potatoes dressed with a smooth and creamy mayonnaise dressing.

Preparation time
10 minutes

Cooking time
35 minutes

Serves
4

Vegetable Soup

Ingredients

2 Medium potatoes (approximately 120 gms), peeled and diced
2 Medium carrots (approximately 120 gms), peeled and diced
½ cup (approx 120 gms) Turnips finely diced
1 Onion finely diced
3 Celery sticks cleaned and diced (approximately 120 gms)
8 Medium tomatoes diced
1000 ml/32 fl oz Water
1 tbsp Olive oil
1 tsp Salt
½ tsp White pepper powder
1 tsp Tabasco sauce (optional)
1 tbsp Cream to garnish

Method

- In a pressure cooker heat the oil. Sauté the onions and celery till translucent.
- Add the carrots, turnips, potatoes and 500 ml water. Pressure cook till vegetables are cooked.
- Blend the tomatoes with 500 ml water in a blender and puree them. Strain the tomato puree to remove tomato seeds.
- Add the tomato puree to the cooked vegetables in the pressure cooker and bring the soup to a boil. Once the soup starts boiling, turn the heat down to allow the soup to simmer, till it reaches the desired consistency. The soup should have a chunky texture but if you prefer smooth soup, you can blend it to a puree after seasoning.
- Season with salt and pepper. Stir in the Tabasco sauce. Adjust seasoning as required.
- Pour into a serving bowl and drizzle over a swirl of cream.

Note: Quantity and choice of vegetables is to personal preference.

Serve with hot crusty bread spread with a generous dollop of garlic butter.

A wonderful, hearty winter soup that is a complete meal in itself.

Preparation time
15 minutes

Cooking time
30 minutes

Serves
4

Leek and Potato Soup

Ingredients

3 Medium potatoes
2 Large leeks
2 tbsp Olive oil

600 ml Vegetable stock
300 ml Milk
1 tsp Salt

1 tsp White pepper
1 Clove garlic minced

Method

- Wash and clean the leeks and chop them into small pieces.
- Peel and dice the potato.
- In a large pan, add the oil and sauté the leeks and garlic till soft and translucent.
- Add the potato and vegetable stock. Bring to a boil, reduce heat and simmer for 20 minutes until vegetables are cooked.
- Season with salt and pepper and stir in the milk. Adjust seasoning as required.
- You can either serve the soup chunky or if you prefer it smooth, blend the soup in a blender to puree it.

Serve with fresh bread.

Rich and creamy leek and potato soup.

Potato Rosti

Ingredients

480 gms / 16 oz Potatoes
60 gms / 2 oz Precooked sweetcorn
1 Small carrot grated

2 Spring onion finely chopped
2 Green chillies finely chopped
1 Red chilli finely chopped

1 tsp Salt
1 tsp White pepper powder
4 tbsp Sunflower oil (for shallow frying)

Preparation time: 20 minutes
Cooking time: 30 minutes
Serves: 4

Method

- Wash and boil the potatoes in water, until ¾ cooked (do not over cook the potatoes).
- Drain the potatoes, peel and put them into the refrigerator to chill.
- In a bowl add sweet corn, grated carrot, spring onion, salt, pepper and the chillies. Mix thoroughly.
- Grate the potatoes on the coarse side of the grater to form long shreds.
- Gently toss the grated potato into the vegetable mixture with very light hands taking care not to mash the potato. You should retain the shape of the shredded potato created by grating.
- Heat a skillet, add little bit of sunflower oil and when it is hot, drop spoonfuls of the potato and vegetable rosti mixture onto the hot oil.
- Allow to cook for 2-3 minutes and then turn over the rosti to cook the second side.
- Once both sides are golden brown remove from pan and keep warm and repeat for rest of the mixture.

Serve as a starter or with salad as a lunch dish.

Savoury crisp potato rosti with a spicy kick.

Preparation time	Cooking time	Serves
15 minutes	20 minutes	4

Chilli Paneer

Ingredients

480 gms/16oz Paneer/Indian cheese diced into 2.5 cm pieces

1 Red capsicum cut into 2.5 cm pieces

1 Green capsicum cut into 2.5 cm pieces

1 Red onion cut into 2.5 cm pieces

1 Red onion finely chopped

4 Green chillies finely chopped

1 tbsp Olive oil to coat paneer pieces

1 tbsp olive oil for sauce

1 tsp Fresh ginger paste

1 tsp Fresh garlic paste

2 tbsp Sun dried tomato paste

2 tbsp Hot chilli sauce

2 tbsp Tomato ketchup

¼ tsp Salt

2 Spring onions slantly cut for garnishing

2 tbsp Dark soya sauce

Finely chopped fresh coriander

Method

- Place the paneer pieces in a bowl and drizzle with 1 tbsp olive oil. Toss and coat the paneer cubes in oil.
- Put paneer pieces on a baking tray and place under a medium grill, turning occasionally to brown all sides (takes 5-10 minutes). Don't over cook, paneer just needs to take the golden colour, otherwise it will be hard to chew.
- Remove paneer cubes from the grill and keep aside.
- Heat 1 tbsp of oil in a wok. Add garlic paste, ginger paste and finely chopped onions. Cook till onions are translucent.
- Add the large pieces of onions, red and green capsicums and finely chopped green chillies. Stir fry vegetables till slightly soft but still crisp and retaining their shape.
- In a jar with a lid add soya sauce, salt, chilli sauce, tomato ketchup and sun dried tomato paste. Place the lid on and shake thoroughly.
- Pour the sauce mixture into the wok over the vegetable mixture and cook till sauce coats all the vegetables and thickens (this takes about five minutes).
- Add the grilled paneer. Toss and coat all paneer pieces thoroughly with the sauce.
- Once the paneer has been heated, transfer to a serving dish. Garnish with finely chopped spring onions and coriander.

Serve warm with a squeeze of lemon juice.

An indo-Chinese fusion of flavours in every mouthful.

Preparation time	Cooking time	Chilling time	Serves
20 minutes (+ 1 hour straining time)	**30 minutes**	**20 minutes**	**4**

Toasted Paneer Rolls

Ingredients

8 Slices bread

240 gms/8 oz Paneer grated

1 Small onion finely chopped

½ tsp Salt

½ tsp Ginger paste

½ tsp Garam masala

1 tbsp Lemon juice

2 Finely minced green chillies

½ tsp Chilli powder

1 tbsp Olive oil for cooking the filling

Spray cooking oil

NB - Garam masala - coriander seeds, cumin seeds, black peppercorns, black cumin seeds, dry ginger powder, cardamom, cloves, cinnamon.

Method

- In a pan, heat 1 tbsp olive oil. When hot, add the onions and cook till soft and translucent.
- Add the ginger paste and chillies.
- Add the grated paneer, followed by the salt, chilli powder, garam masala and lemon juice. Cover and cook the paneer for 5 minutes.
- Take off heat and cool.
- Divide the paneer masala into 8 portions. Roll each one into a sausage shape to fit the width of the bread slice. Chill for 15-30 minutes.
- Remove the crusts from the bread slices.
- Using a rolling pin, roll out the bread slices to flatten them.
- Place the paneer masala sausage on the bread roll at one end, and roll up the bread slice tightly.
- Wet the other end of the bread slice and stick it down to form a sausage shape.
- Repeat the process for all bread slices.
- Spray a baking tray with spray oil and place paneer bread rolls on it (you can use ordinary oil and just brush the bread rolls over with it instead).
- Spray the bread rolls with the spray oil and bake in a preheated oven at 200°C / 400°F for 20 minutes or until golden brown.

Remove from oven and serve with coriander chutney.

Spicy paneer filling encased in bread slices to form rolled toasted bread sandwiches.

Preparation time
15 minutes

Cooking time
20 minutes

Serves
4

Mushroom Masala Rolls

Ingredients

- 12 Button mushrooms
- 1 Small red onion
- 120 gms/4 oz Frozen peas
- 2 Green chillies finely chopped
- ½ tsp Garlic paste
- ¼ tsp Salt
- 1 tbsp Soya sauce
- ½ tbsp Sweet chilli sauce
- ½ tbsp Tomato ketchup
- 2 tbsp Olive oil

For serving:
- 4 Bread buns
- 1 tbsp Butter

Method

- Clean the mushrooms and chop finely.
- Peel the onion and chop finely.
- Put the peas in boiling water for 3 minutes to defrost them and then drain and keep aside.
- In a wok add olive oil and allow to heat. Add onions and garlic and sauté till translucent. Add mushrooms and peas and sauté for 5 minutes till mushroom and peas are cooked.
- Add green chillies, soya sauce, salt, chilli sauce and tomato ketchup.
- Sauté the mushroom masala for 2-3 minutes further till all the sauce and mushroom mixture infuses together.
- Cut the bread rolls in half and butter them.
- Heat a frying pan, when hot, place the bread rolls buttered side down to slightly toast them.
- Remove the toasted bread roll halves and place on a serving dish. Generously spoon the mushroom masala on top.

Serve hot immediately.

Open topped bread rolls with a delicious Indo–Chinese mushroom topping making it a substantial dish for either lunch or breakfast.

Preparation time
1 hour

Cooking time
20 minutes

Makes
8

Lentil Pancakes

Ingredients

240 gms/ 8 oz Split moong dhal with husk
375 ml / 12 fl oz Water
2 tbsp Natural yoghurt
1 tsp Eno salt
1 tsp Salt
½ tsp Turmeric powder
1 tsp Fresh ginger paste
2 Green chillies finely chopped
½ cup Fresh fenugreek chopped
3 Spring onions finely chopped
3 tbsp Sunflower oil

Method

- Wash the moong dhal and soak for 1 hour. After soaking drain the water from it and put into a blender
- Add salt, turmeric, ginger paste, chillies and fenugreek.
- Add the measured water and yoghurt. Blend to form a dropping consistency batter.
- Stir in the chopped spring onions and eno salt.
- Heat a frying pan and oil it. Place a ladle full of mixture and spread it to form a small pancake, (these pancakes are thicker and smaller than average pancake).
- Once the pancake batter starts to set flip the pancake over and cook the underside.
- Place on kitchen paper and repeat process for rest of the batter.

Serve with yoghurt and pickle.

Healthy, protein packed and simply delicious savoury pancakes flavoured with spring onions and fenugreek.

Preparation time
15 minutes

Cooking time
30 minutes

Serves
4

Spinach Fritters

Ingredients

120 gms/4 oz Chickpea flour
30 gms/1 oz Rice flour
1 tsp Fresh ginger paste
1 tsp Green chilli paste
¾ tsp (or to taste) Salt

½ tsp Chilli powder
1 tsp Turmeric powder
½ tsp Carom seeds
½ tsp Eno salt
3 tbsp Water

3 Thinly sliced Spring onions
1 Cup mixed green /red/ yellow peppers cut into thin 2.5 cm slices
480 gms/16 oz Fresh spinach chopped coarsely
600 ml /20 fl oz Sunflower oil for deep frying

Method

- Mix rice flour and chickpea flour. Add turmeric, salt, chilli powder, carom seeds, ginger and chilli paste to it.
- Add water and make a paste.
- Add the peppers, onions and chopped spinach. Mix to make a dropping consistency batter. Add a little more water if needed.
- Add eno salt and mix thoroughly.

- Heat the oil. Once the oil is hot, drop spoonfuls of batter into the hot oil. Deep fry on medium heat till fritters are golden brown and crispy.
- Remove from oil and drain on kitchen paper.
- Repeat procedure for rest of the batter.

Serve hot with chilli sauce.

A colourful medley of spinach, peppers and onions coated in a spicy batter and deep fried to make a mouth watering tea time snack.

Preparation time
10 minutes

Cooking time
30 minutes

Makes
12

Serves
6

Spicy Savoury Pancakes

Ingredients

240 gms/8 oz Chickpea flour
60 gms/2 oz Fresh fenugreek finely chopped
1½ tsp Salt

2-3 Green chillies finely chopped
1 tsp Fresh ginger paste
1 tsp Oil
½ tsp Eno salt

½ tsp Chilli powder (optional)
2 tbsp Oil for cooking pancakes
8 fl oz/250 ml Water to make batter

For dressing:
120 gms/4 oz Natural yoghurt
2 tbsp Coriander chutney

Method

- Put the water, chick pea flour, chillies, ginger, fenugreek leaves and salt in a blender. Make a thin batter.
- To this batter, add 1 tsp oil and eno salt. Stir well.
- Heat a non-stick skillet or frying pan and sparingly oil it. Using a ladle, pour some batter on to the hot skillet and spread in a circular motion using the back of the ladle to form a thin pancake.
- When bubbles start to form on the pancake, lightly spread oil on to it and flip it over. Cook other side for about 2-3 minutes.
- Pancake is ready, when it turns slightly brown and batter is fully set.
- Repeat for the remaining batter.

To serve:

- Mix the coriander chutney with natural yoghurt and make a dip.
- Spread the dip over the pancakes and roll them up like a Swiss roll.

Serve immediately.

A savoury pancake made from chickpea flour and fresh fenugreek.

Preparation time
10 minutes

Cooking time
5-10 minutes

Serves
2

Triple Decker Spicy Sandwich

Ingredients

8 Slices boiled potato
8 Slices tomato
8 Slices cucumber

6 Slices bread
3 tbsp Coriander chutney
1 Red chilli finely chopped

¼ tsp Salt
Few red onion rings

Method

- Remove the crust from all six slices of bread.
- Place two slices of bread side by side on a tray to make two sandwiches.
- Spread coriander chutney onto the bread slices and place the cucumber on top.
- On top of the cucumber slices add the potato slices and sprinkle with red chillies and a little more coriander chutney. Season with salt and pepper.
- Place the second slice of bread on top of the potato slices on both sandwiches.
- Spread coriander chutney on top of this slice and add tomato slices and finally the onion rings with a little more coriander chutney.
- Add the third slice of bread on each sandwich.
- Cut the sandwiches diagonally so that you have 4 sandwiches.

Serve immediately with potato chips.

Hearty sandwich with flavours of the east. It is a three layered sandwich topped with a variety of fillings and laced with spicy and tangy coriander chutney.

Preparation time
20 minutes

Cooking time
15-20 minutes

Serves
2

Onion Fritters

Ingredients

1 Large onion
1 tsp Salt
½ tsp Chilli powder
½ tsp Eno salt
180 gms/6 oz Chickpea flour
1 tbsp Semolina
1 tsp Ginger paste
3-4 Green chillies finely chopped
1 tsp Turmeric powder
2-3 tbsp Water
1 tbsp Fresh chopped coriander
600 ml/20 fl oz Sunflower Oil for frying

Method

- In a bowl, add the chickpea flour and semolina. Mix thoroughly.
- Add the salt, chilli powder, chillies, turmeric, ginger paste and eno salt to the chickpea flour. Mix and keep aside.
- Slice the onions into thin slices and separate them.
- In a bowl, add chopped coriander and onion slices. Sprinkle spiced flour mixture on top of the onions. Toss to coat the onions thoroughly with the spiced flour. Sprinkle 2-3 tbsp of water to help the flour mixture stick to the onions. The mixture should not be too wet.
- Divide the mixture into 8 parts and shape into rough patties and place on a floured tray.
- Heat the oil in a pan to medium hot.
- Drop the onion patties four at a time into the oil and fry on medium heat till golden brown (do not cook on too high heat otherwise fritters will remain uncooked inside).
- Remove from oil when golden brown and drain on kitchen paper.
- Repeat process for remainder.
- Transfer fritters to a serving dish.

Serve with ketchup, chilli sauce or any chutney of choice.

Hot crispy onion fritters make a delectable spicy crunch in every mouthful. A perfect tea time snack.

Snacks - Indian/Chinese Themed Recipes | 55

Preparation time
15 minutes

Cooking time
10 minutes

Chilling time
45 minutes

Serves
2

Spicy Potato Cakes

Ingredients

240 gms/8 oz Boiled and mashed potato
60 gms/2 oz Green peas boiled, coarsely ground
1/2 tsp Fresh ginger paste
2 Green chillies finely chopped

1 tsp Salt
½ tsp Chilli powder
2 Spring onions finely chopped
1 tsp Garam masala
8 Slices white bread

4 tbsp Oil for shallow frying
NB - Garam masala - coriander seeds, cumin seeds, black peppercorns, black cumin seeds, dry ginger powder, cardamom, cloves, cinnamon.

Method

- In a bowl add the mashed potato, coarsely ground boiled peas, spring onions, green chillies and ginger paste. Mix together.
- Add salt, chilli powder, garam masala and mix thoroughly.
- Divide the mixture into 8 parts. Roll each part into a round ball. Cover and place in the refrigerator to chill for 15 minutes.
- Cut the crusts of the bread slices and keep the bread slices aside.
- In a shallow dish put some water, dip each bread slice in the water to dampen it but do not over soak the bread slice.
- Place the potato ball in the centre of the damp bread slice and gather the sides of the bread slice together in the centre to encase the potato mixture to form a ball.
- Tightly press together the edges of the bread slice to seal the potato mixture in the bread slice to form a tikki (potato cake). Flatten the tikki between the palms of your hands.
- Repeat procedure for remaining bread slices. Chill the tikkis again for 30 minutes.
- In frying pan, add some oil and heat on medium heat. When the oil is hot, shallow fry the tikkis till golden brown on both sides.

Serve hot garnished with some salad. Use tomato ketchup or chilli sauce as a dip.

A fast and easy snack of spiced potato mixture encased in a bread covering.

Preparation time
20 minutes

Chilling time
30 minutes

Serves
4

Spicy Fruit Salad

Ingredients

1 Apple diced
1 Pear diced
2 Nectarines or peaches deseeded and diced
10 Green grapes
10 Black grapes
1 Firm ripe mango deseeded and diced
Passion fruit seeds from 4 passion fruits

For dressing:
3 tbsp Orange juice
1/2 tsp Chaat masala for dressing
1/2 tsp Chaat masala for sprinkling on top of fruit salad
A pinch of White pepper
A pinch of Salt

NB - Chaat Masala - dried mango powder, cumin powder, black salt, coriander powder, dried ginger powder, salt, black pepper, asafoetida and chilli powder.

Method

- Put all the prepared fruit into a bowl and mix.
- In a screw top jar add the orange juice, pepper powder salt and chaat masala. Cover with lid. Shake to mix the dressing.
- Pour the dressing over the fruit and mix thoroughly. Chill fruit salad for 30 minutes.
- Spoon the fruit salad into serving bowls and sprinkle with a pinch of chaat masala.

Perfect for that hot summer day. This colourful spicy fruit salad is seasoned with a spicy chaat masala. It is a cooling and refreshing treat.

Snacks - Indian/Chinese Themed Recipes

Preparation time
10 minutes

Cooking time
20-30 minutes

Serves
4

Barbecue Roasted Corn Salad

Ingredients

4 Whole corns on the cob
1 Finely chopped small red onion
60 gms/2 oz Finely diced mixed capsicums
½ tsp Chilli powder
½ tsp Salt

½ tsp Chaat masala
1 tbsp Fresh chopped coriander
2 tbsp Thin pieces of fried gram snack
Juice of half a lemon

NB- Chaat Masala - dried mango powder, cumin powder, black salt, coriander powder, dried ginger powder, salt, black pepper, asafoetida and chilli powder.

Method

- Roast the corn on the cob on the barbecue or under grill till it is slightly charred and cooked. Keep rotating it at intervals to ensure even cooking.
- Using a sharp knife remove the corn kernels from the barbecued corn and put into a bowl.
- Add diced onion, diced capsicum and mix thoroughly.

Serve immediately.

- Drizzle the corn with lemon juice and add salt, chilli powder and chaat masala. Mix well.
- Transfer to a serving dish and sprinkle pieces of fried gram snack and chopped coriander on top of the corn salad before serving.

A wonderful outdoor taste of barbecue roasted fresh corn on the cob with multicoloured sweet peppers and sweet red onion.

Preparation time
10 minutes

Cooking time
5 minutes

Serves
4

Green Bean Salad

Ingredients

240 gms/8 oz Long green beans
1 tbsp Pine nuts
1 Red Chilli finely chopped
¼ tsp Salt
¼ tsp Pepper powder
1 tbsp Olive oil
1 tbsp Lemon juice
Parmesan shavings

Method

- Top and tail the green beans. Blanch them in salted water for 5 minutes.
- Drain the beans and drop them into iced water to stop them from cooking further.
- Drain the cooked green beans from the iced water and transfer them to a bowl.
- In a frying pan, dry toast the pine nuts till golden brown.
- Add to the green beans salt, black pepper, olive oil, red chilli and lemon juice.
- Toss the green beans so that they are well coated with the dressing.
- Transfer green bean salad to a serving dish and sprinkle with the toasted pine nuts and parmesan shavings.
- Serve immediately.

Parmesan shavings and toasted pine nuts lavishly sprinkled on top of tender green beans.

Preparation time
5 minutes

Cooking time
10 minutes

Serves
2

Cheesy Savoury French Toast

Ingredients

4 Slices white bread
2 Eggs
30 gms/1 oz Cheddar cheese finely grated
60 ml/2 fl oz Milk
¼ tsp Salt
¼ tsp Pepper
½ tbsp Fresh chopped coriander
1 tbsp Finely chopped chives
1 Green chilli finely chopped
1 tbsp Each butter & olive oil

Method

- Cut the bread slices into the desired shape (triangle or heart shaped with cookie cutter). Keep aside.
- In a bowl add milk, eggs, salt, pepper, coriander, chives, chilli and pepper. Mix thoroughly and stir in the cheese.
- Put butter and olive oil in a frying pan.
- Dip each piece of bread into the egg mixture and place in the hot frying pan. Cook on both sides till bread is golden brown.
- Transfer to a serving dish and repeat for rest of the bread slices.

Serve savoury toast with baked beans for breakfast or with soup for lunch.

A tasty snack that is versatile, mouth watering and simple to make. The combination of cheese and chives gives this French toast an extra heartiness.

Preparation time
10 minutes

Cooking time
50 minutes

Serves
4

Onion Soup

Ingredients

2 Large onions
1000 ml/32 fl oz Water
2 tbsp Corn flour

1 tbsp Olive oil
30 gms/1 oz Butter
60 gms/2 oz Gruyere cheese

4 Slices french bread
1 tsp Salt
½ tsp White pepper powder

Method

- Finely slice the onions.
- In a large pot add the olive oil and butter. When butter starts to froth, add the onion slices and cook on a very low heat for 30 minutes. This is important as the onions need to be cooked slowly to caramelize.
- After 30 minutes, add water and bring to a boil. Turn down the heat and allow soup to simmer.
- Take 4 tbsp of liquid from the soup pan and mix with the cornflour in a cup ensuring there are no lumps.
- Add this cornflour mixture to the soup and mix it thoroughly.
- Season the soup with salt and pepper and simmer for another 10-15 minutes. The cornflour will make soup slightly thicker. Adjust seasoning as required.

To serve:

- Top the French bread slices with the cheese and place under a hot grill to brown. Once the cheese has browned, remove bread from grill.
- Ladle the soup into soup bowls and float one slice of cheesy bread on top of the hot soup.
- Serve immediately.

Slow cooking of the caramelised onion gives this soup a unique sweetness. Hearty and delicious, it makes a perfect lunch starter.

Preparation time
15 minutes

Cooking time
25 minutes

Serves
2

Garlic Mushrooms

Ingredients

- 60 gms / 2 oz Bread crumbs
- 30 gms / 1 oz Grated cheddar cheese
- 2 Spring onions finely chopped
- 1 tsp Garlic paste
- ¼ tsp Salt
- ¼ tsp black pepper
- 1 tbsp fresh Parsley, finely chopped
- 4 Large mushrooms
- 1 tbsp Olive oil

Method

- Preheat the oven to 180°C / 375°F.
- Wipe the mushrooms clean with a damp cloth, remove the stalks and place the mushrooms on an oiled baking tray.
- In a bowl, add the breadcrumbs, garlic paste, salt, pepper, parsley, spring onions and the grated cheese. Mix well.
- Spoon the mixture into the centre of the 4 mushrooms. Drizzle with a little olive oil.
- Place the filled mushrooms in the preheated oven for 20-25 minutes till the breadcrumb mixture starts to look golden and toasted.

Remove from oven and serve with a side salad.

Garlicky cheesy breadcrumb mixture topped mushrooms.

Weight Conversions

Imperial	Metric	US cups
1 oz	30 grams	
4 oz	120 grams	½ cup
8 oz	240 grams	1 cup
16 oz	480 grams	2 cups

Liquid Conversions

Imperial	Metric	US cups
½ fl oz	15 ml	1 tbsp
1 fl oz	30 ml	
4 fl oz	125 ml	½ cup
8 fl oz	250 ml	1 cup
16 fl oz	500 ml	2 cups
20 fl oz (1 pint)	600 ml	2 ½ cups
33 fl oz (1 litre)		

Oven temperature Conversions

Fahrenheit - °F	Centigrade - °C	Gas
225	110	¼
250	120	½
275	140	1
300	150	2
325	160	3
350	175	4
375	190	5
400	200	6
425	220	7
450	230	8
475	240	9
500	260	10

Notes

All cooking times given in the book are approximate; they may vary slightly with different types of cookers, grills, hobs and microwaves used.

Ratio of water given in making rice and dough can vary depending on different brands used. Water measurements are approximate and a minor adjustment in quantity used may be required.

Index

A
Apple and sweet onion salsa 15
Avocado dip 13

B
Barbecue roasted corn salad 58
Bruschetta 23

C
Cheesy savoury French toast 60
Chickpea and mango salad 20
Chilli paneer 47
Chilli salsa and wheat tortilla chips 11

E
Egg and cress sandwiches 39
English cucumber sandwich 38

G
Garlic mushrooms 62
Garlic paprika potato wedges 7
Grape and carrot salad 35
Green bean salad 59

H
Hot ribboned omelette salad 34

K
Kidney beans and sweet corn pitta pockets 14
Kids delight – strawberry jam sandwich 41

L
Leek and potato soup 44

M
Macaroni cheese 33
Mexican quesadillas 17
Lentil pancakes 51
Moroccan couscous salad 27
Moroccan vegetarian harira soup 29
Mushroom masala rolls 50

N
New potato salad 42

O
Onion fritters 55
Onion soup 61
Oven roasted tomato and basil soup 24

P
Penne arrabbiata 25
Potato chip sticks 30
Potato rosti 45
Potato skins 31

R
Red cabbage & apple relish 32
Rice salad 8
Roasted vegetables in pitta bread pockets 21

S
Scrambled egg tortilla wraps 12
Sour cream and chive dip 26
Spicy fruit salad 57
Spicy potato cakes 56
Spicy savoury pancakes 53
Spinach fritters 52
Sprouted moong bean salad 09

T
Toasted cheese, tomato and onion sandwich 40
Toasted paneer rolls 48
Triple decker spicy sandwich 54
Tropical fruit salad with honey and lime dressing 19
Tzatziki cucumber and yoghurt dip 22

V
Vegetable burgers 37
Vegetable kebabs 18
Vegetable soup 43

SNACKS

First Edition: 2013
1st Impression: 2013

All rights reserved. No part of this book may be reproduced, stored in a retrieval system or transmitted, in any form or by any means, mechanical, photocopying, recording or otherwise, without any prior written permission of the publisher.

© with the author

Published by Kuldeep Jain for

HEALTH HARMONY
An imprint of
B. JAIN PUBLISHERS (P) LTD.
1921/10, Chuna Mandi, Paharganj, New Delhi 110 055 (INDIA)
Tel.: +91-11-4567 1000 • Fax: +91-11-4567 1010
Email: info@bjain.com • Website: www.bjain.com

Printed in India by
JJ Imprints Pvt. Ltd.

ISBN: 978-81-319-1134-1